Disclaimer

This book, *Unlocking X's (Twitter) Potential: Step-by-Step Methods to Grow and Monetize Your Presence,* is designed to provide educational and informational insights into building and monetizing a presence on X (formerly known as Twitter). The author and publisher have made every effort to ensure the accuracy and relevance of the information presented, but no guarantees are made regarding the completeness, timeliness, or applicability of the strategies to every reader's unique circumstances.

Content Accuracy and Relevance

Social media platforms like X are dynamic, with features, policies, monetization tools, and algorithms subject to change. While this book reflects the platform's state at the time of writing, readers should regularly consult X's official resources, updates, and terms of service for the latest information. The author and publisher are not responsible for any discrepancies or outdated content.

No Guarantee of Success

The strategies and examples outlined in this book are based on best practices and case studies from successful creators. However, individual results will vary depending on numerous factors, including niche, audience engagement, effort, and market conditions. This book does not guarantee financial success, follower growth, or other specific outcomes.

Professional Advice Disclaimer

The content in this book should not be interpreted as professional advice in areas such as finance, legal compliance, or business operations. Readers should seek guidance from qualified professionals in these fields before making decisions that may impact their financial, legal, or professional standing.

Limitations of Liability

The author and publisher disclaim any liability for direct or indirect damages, losses, or issues arising from the application of the strategies in this book. By reading and implementing the content, you acknowledge that you are solely responsible for the results and outcomes of your actions.

Third-Party References

This book may reference third-party tools, services, or platforms to illustrate strategies or provide additional resources. These references are for informational purposes only, and the author and publisher do not endorse or assume responsibility for their functionality, reliability, or compliance. Readers should independently assess the suitability of any third-party resources.

Earnings Disclaimer

Examples of income or monetization provided in this book are for illustrative purposes only and should not be construed as promises or guarantees of financial results. Success in monetization depends on many factors, including individual effort, strategy execution, and audience engagement.

Trademarks and Affiliations

"X," "Twitter," and related logos or branding are trademarks of their respective owners. This book is not affiliated with, endorsed by, or associated with X, Twitter, or its parent company. The use of these names is for descriptive purposes only.

By using this book, you agree to this disclaimer and accept full responsibility for your actions and decisions based on the information provided. The author and publisher recommend using discretion and adapting the content to suit your individual goals and circumstances.

TABLE OF CONTENT

Book Description

Unlocking X's (Twitter) Potential: Step-by-Step Methods to Grow and Monetize Your Presence

Are you ready to transform your presence on X (formerly Twitter) into a thriving platform for growth and income? Whether you're a creator, entrepreneur, or professional, *Unlocking X's (Twitter) Potential* is your ultimate guide to mastering the art of building an engaged audience and monetizing your content.

This comprehensive step-by-step book covers everything you need to know about succeeding on X, from optimizing your profile and creating engaging content to leveraging the platform's monetization features and navigating its ever-evolving landscape. Drawing on real-world examples and actionable strategies, this book is packed with insights to help you achieve your goals, whether that's growing a loyal following, earning ad revenue, or launching your own products and services.

What You'll Learn

- Build a Magnetic Profile: Create a professional and engaging presence that attracts followers and opportunities.
- Master Content Creation: Develop a content strategy that resonates with your audience, from viral threads to multimedia posts.
- Explore Monetization Strategies: Tap into features like ad revenue sharing, subscriptions, affiliate marketing, and sponsored content.
- Navigate Challenges and Risks: Handle negative interactions, protect your account, and balance mental well-being.
- Stay Ahead of Changes: Adapt to new trends, platform updates, and algorithm shifts to maintain your competitive edge.
- Achieve Growth Milestones: Discover proven strategies to hit 5 million impressions in just 30 days.

Who This Book Is For

- Content creators looking to monetize their efforts.
- Entrepreneurs and brands wanting to leverage X for marketing and community building.
- Social media enthusiasts eager to understand and maximize the platform's potential.

Featuring inspiring case studies, expert tips, and practical tools, *Unlocking X's (Twitter) Potential* is the roadmap to turning your presence on X into a sustainable and profitable venture. Whether you're starting from scratch or refining your strategy, this book will empower you to succeed in the ever-changing world of social media.

Start your journey to success on X today!

Chapter 1: Understanding X and Its Monetization Landscape

X, formerly known as Twitter, stands as one of the most dynamic social media platforms, evolving from a microblogging service into a robust ecosystem for creators, businesses, and users alike. Under Elon Musk's leadership, X has undergone a significant transformation, introducing innovative monetization opportunities and reshaping how creators can build and sustain their presence online. This chapter offers a comprehensive look at X's evolution, its current monetization strategies, and the foundational steps required to thrive in this new era.

1.1 The Evolution of X

The rebranding of Twitter to X in **July 2023** marked a pivotal moment in the platform's history. This transformation signaled Elon Musk's vision of turning Twitter into an "everything app," blending traditional social networking with a suite of services ranging from payments to video and beyond.

Key milestones in X's evolution include:

- **Logo Transformation**: The iconic blue bird, synonymous with Twitter for over a decade, was replaced by a bold, stylized "X," reflecting a new brand identity.
- **Domain Shift**: Twitter's domain transitioned from **twitter.com** to **x.com**, underscoring the platform's shift towards Musk's ambitious goals.
- **Full Rebranding by 2024**: By May 2024, the rebranding was complete, cementing X's position as a platform of the future.

This evolution has redefined the way users and creators interact with the platform, offering exciting possibilities while also introducing unique challenges. For content creators, the shift opens new doors for monetization but requires a keen understanding of the platform's mechanics and its changing user demographics.

1.2 Current Monetization Strategies on X

X offers creators multiple avenues to generate income, focusing on fostering engagement and rewarding impactful content. Below are the primary monetization features available:

1. **Creator Revenue Sharing Program**
   Initially designed to pay creators based on ad impressions in replies, this

program shifted in **November 2024** to reward engagement from **X Premium users**. This model prioritizes creators who generate content that resonates deeply with subscribers, emphasizing interaction and relevance. *Example*: A creator who frequently posts engaging threads, polls, or thought-provoking content that garners attention from X Premium users will see higher revenue than someone with sporadic or low-engagement posts.

2. **X   Premium   Subscriptions**
Creators can offer exclusive content to their subscribers for a monthly fee, typically ranging from **$2.99 to $9.99**. This feature allows creators to establish a steady income stream while fostering a closer relationship with their most loyal followers.
Example: A fitness coach might share detailed workout plans and behind-the-scenes videos exclusively with subscribers, providing them unique value while generating consistent income.

3. **Tips   and   Donations**
The Tips feature enables followers to directly support creators with one-time payments. This is ideal for creators who produce highly appreciated free content, such as art, tutorials, or motivational threads.
Example: An illustrator sharing free artwork might include a "Tip" button, allowing appreciative fans to contribute financially as a token of gratitude.

1.3 Establishing a Monetizable Presence

To successfully monetize on X, creators must lay a strong foundation by focusing on key elements:

1. **Profile Optimization**
   - **Profile Picture**: Use a professional and recognizable image that reflects your personal or brand identity.
   - **Bio**: Craft a concise and impactful bio that clearly communicates who you are and what you offer. For instance, a content creator might write: "Helping creators grow & monetize on X | DM for collabs."
   - **Header Image**: Use this space creatively to promote your brand, showcase achievements, or display contact information.
2. *Example*: A tech blogger could use their header image to highlight a popular blog post, link to their website, or share their subscription offerings.
3. **Content   Strategy**
Consistency is key. Develop a clear posting schedule that aligns with your niche and target audience. Prioritize high-quality content that provides value, whether through education, entertainment, or inspiration.
Example: A personal finance coach might post daily tips, host weekly Q&A sessions, and create monthly in-depth threads on saving strategies.
4. **Engagement**
Actively interact with your audience by responding to comments, joining trending discussions, and collaborating with other creators. Engaging authentically with your followers builds trust and fosters a loyal community.

5. **Compliance**   **with**   **Policies**
Familiarize yourself with X's content guidelines and monetization policies to avoid potential penalties, such as demonetization or account suspension.

1.4 Navigating the Transition to Engagement-Based Earnings

The move towards an **engagement-based earnings model** requires creators to adapt their approach. Here's how you can thrive under the new system:

1. **Understanding**   **X**   **Premium**   **Users**
   Engagement from X Premium users now directly impacts revenue. Learn about this demographic—what they value, their preferred types of content, and how they interact with posts. For example, X Premium users might favor thought leadership, exclusive insights, or timely news.
2. **Encouraging**   **Meaningful**   **Interactions**
   Create content that sparks discussions or encourages users to share and comment. Consider asking open-ended questions or addressing trending topics relevant   to   your   niche.
   Example: A travel blogger might post, "What's the best off-the-beaten-path destination you've visited? Let me know!" to spark a conversation.
3. **Monitoring**   **Performance**   **Metrics**
   Leverage X's analytics tools to track performance. Identify which posts are driving the most engagement and adjust your strategy accordingly.
   Example: If analytics show higher engagement for videos over text posts, focus on producing more video content to maximize earnings.

Conclusion

X's evolution into a dynamic platform for creators presents unparalleled opportunities to monetize content and grow a personal brand. By understanding its current monetization landscape and taking proactive steps to build a strong presence, creators can unlock the platform's full potential. As we move through the book, we'll explore detailed strategies and actionable tips to help you make the most of your journey on X.

Chapter 2: Setting Up and Optimizing Your X Profile

Your profile on X (formerly Twitter) is your digital calling card—a powerful first impression that shapes how others perceive and interact with you. Whether you're a content creator, a business, or an individual building your brand, setting up a professional and engaging profile is essential for attracting followers and achieving your monetization goals. This chapter provides a step-by-step guide to creating and optimizing your X profile for maximum impact.

2.1 Creating Your X Account

Sign Up

- Visit X's official website or download the app.
- Click on **"Sign Up"** and provide the necessary details, including:
    - Your name.
    - A valid phone number or email address.
    - A strong, secure password.

Username Selection

Your username, also known as your handle, is one of the most recognizable elements of your profile. Make it:

- **Reflective of your brand or niche**: Sports fans often incorporate identifiers like "Utd" for Manchester United, "CFC" for Chelsea, or "DCB" for Dallas Cowboys. Cryptocurrency enthusiasts might use "Crypto" or terms like "BTC" in their usernames.
- **Short and memorable**: A concise handle is easier for others to remember and share. For example, @FitnessGuru or @CryptoPro.
- **Consistent across platforms**: Use the same username on other social media to strengthen your online identity.

2.2 Profile Picture

Importance

Your profile picture is the first thing users notice. It's a crucial element of your brand identity. For individuals, it might be a headshot; for businesses, it could be your logo.

Specifications

- **Size**: 400x400 pixels for optimal quality.
- **Clarity**: Ensure the image is clear and recognizable, even in smaller formats.
- **Brand alignment**: Use colors and imagery that align with your brand aesthetic.

Example: A personal finance coach might use a professional headshot with a neutral background, while a coffee shop could showcase its logo against a vibrant coffee-themed design.

2.3 Header Image

Purpose

Your header image provides a larger canvas for branding. It's ideal for:

- Highlighting key products or services.
- Showcasing achievements, such as awards or partnerships.
- Promoting an upcoming event or campaign.

Specifications

- **Size**: 1500x500 pixels.
- **Design tips**: Maintain simplicity and ensure the design doesn't clash with your profile picture or text.

Example: A musician could use the header to promote their latest album, while a tech brand might display a tagline like "Innovating the Future."

2.4 Crafting Your Bio

Your bio is a 160-character introduction that explains who you are, what you do, and what you offer.

Tips for Writing a Great Bio

- **Highlight your niche**: Use clear keywords. For example, "Fitness Coach | Helping busy professionals stay healthy" or "Tech Enthusiast | AI & Blockchain Insights."
- **Include a CTA**: Encourage specific actions, such as "DM for collaborations" or "Visit my website for free resources."
- **Be authentic**: Show personality to connect with your audience.

Example: A travel blogger might write: "Exploring the world, one city at a time | Travel tips & vlogs | Subscribe for exclusive guides."

2.5 Website Link

Utilization

X allows one link in your profile. Use this space strategically to drive traffic to:

- Your personal website.
- A newsletter subscription page.
- A landing page for a product or campaign.

Pro Tip

Consider using tools like **Bitly** or **Linktree** to create a custom, trackable link and include multiple destinations if needed.

2.6 Location

Adding your location builds trust and helps followers connect with you.

- **For local businesses**: Mention your primary city or area of operation.
- **For global creators**: Indicate a worldwide presence or omit the location if unnecessary.

Example: A freelance designer might list "Remote | Available Worldwide," while a coffee shop could say "Seattle, WA."

2.7 Pinned Tweet

Purpose

A pinned tweet remains at the top of your profile, making it ideal for highlighting:

- Announcements.
- Best-performing content.
- Promotional offers.

Best Practices

- Keep it updated to reflect current goals.
- Include a clear **Call-to-Action (CTA)** like "Sign up now!" or "Check out my latest blog."

Example: A nonprofit might pin a tweet about a fundraising campaign, while a content creator could showcase their most viral thread.

2.8 Profile Optimization Tips

1. **Consistency**
   Maintain uniform branding across your profile picture, header image, bio, and content. This makes your brand instantly recognizable.
2. **Keyword**   **Integration**
   Use niche-specific keywords in your bio and tweets to improve discoverability in search results.
3. **Hashtags**
   Research and incorporate trending and relevant hashtags in your content to increase visibility. For instance, a food blogger could use #Foodie, #RecipeOfTheDay, or #HealthyEating.
4. **Engagement**
   Actively respond to comments, retweet relevant content, and join discussions. Engaging with your audience builds community and encourages more followers.

2.9 Compliance with X Policies

Adherence

Ensure your profile and content comply with X's guidelines, which prohibit:

- Spam.
- Harassment.
- Copyright infringement.

Verification

If eligible, apply for verification to add credibility. Verified accounts are marked with a **blue checkmark**, signaling authenticity.

Conclusion

Optimizing your X profile is the first step to building a powerful presence on the platform. A well-crafted profile not only attracts followers but also sets the stage for monetization by showcasing your brand's value. In the next chapter, we'll explore X's monetization features in detail, helping you turn your optimized profile into a revenue-generating tool.

Chapter 3: Building a Strong Personal Brand on X

Establishing a personal brand on X (formerly Twitter) is a cornerstone of audience growth and monetization. Your personal brand is more than just a logo or tagline—it's the identity, values, and unique value you offer your audience. On X, where the competition for attention is fierce, a compelling and authentic personal brand helps you stand out, build trust, and create lasting connections. This chapter guides you step-by-step in crafting and enhancing your personal brand on X.

3.1 Understanding Personal Branding

Personal branding is about shaping how others perceive you. It combines your identity, values, and expertise into a consistent, memorable image. A strong personal brand on X can lead to:

- **Audience Growth**: Attract followers who align with your niche and values.
- **Higher Engagement**: Build deeper connections through authentic interactions.
- **Monetization Opportunities**: Appeal to brands, collaborators, and supporters looking for influencers with credibility.

Example: Elon Musk's presence on X showcases his unique brand—innovative, bold, and unfiltered. His tweets resonate with his audience because they align with his brand identity.

3.2 Defining Your Brand Identity

1. **Identify Your Niche**
   Focus on specific topics or industries where you have expertise or passion. Specializing allows you to attract a targeted audience.
   Example: A tech enthusiast might focus on AI, blockchain, or gadget reviews. A fitness influencer could target busy professionals with quick, effective workouts.
2. **Clarify Your Value Proposition**
   Determine what sets you apart. What unique insights or value can you offer your audience? Examples include:
   - Expert advice or tutorials.
   - Personal stories and perspectives.
   - Entertaining or thought-provoking content.
3. *Example*: A digital marketing expert could offer actionable tips on SEO or share case studies of successful campaigns.

4. **Establish Your Brand Voice**
Your tone and style should reflect your personality and resonate with your audience. Choose a consistent voice—be it professional, humorous, casual, or inspirational.
Example: A sustainability advocate might use a hopeful and motivating tone, while a comedian might focus on humor and wit.

3.3 Optimizing Your X Profile

A polished profile reinforces your personal brand. Here's how to make each element count:

1. **Profile Picture**
Use a high-quality image that reflects your brand. For personal brands, a clear, professional headshot works best.
2. **Header Image**
Select a header that complements your profile picture and represents your brand. It could showcase your tagline, products, or a compelling image related to your niche.
Example: A travel blogger could feature an image of a scenic destination, while a startup founder might use a clean design with their company logo.
3. **Bio**
Craft a concise and impactful bio:
   ○ Highlight your expertise and interests.
   ○ Use relevant keywords for discoverability.
   ○ Include a clear call-to-action (CTA), like "DM for inquiries" or "Join my newsletter."
   Example: "Sustainability advocate | Tips for a greener life | DM for collabs ."
4. **Pinned Tweet**
Feature a tweet that introduces new followers to your brand or highlights your best content.
Example: Pin a tweet that links to your most popular thread or announces a new project.

3.4 Developing a Content Strategy

Your content strategy should align with your brand identity and audience's interests.

1. **Content Pillars**
Define 3-5 core themes around which your content revolves. These could include:
   ○ Tutorials or "how-to" guides.
   ○ Industry insights or trends.
   ○ Personal stories or behind-the-scenes content.

2. *Example*: A fitness creator might focus on workout tips, nutrition advice, and motivational posts.
3. **Content** **Calendar**
Plan your posts to maintain consistency. Use tools like **ClickUp**, **Notion**, or **Buffer** to organize and schedule your content.
4. **Content** **Types**
Mix up your posts to keep your audience engaged:
    o Short tweets for quick insights or tips.
    o Threads for in-depth content.
    o Images and videos for visual impact.
    o Polls to encourage interaction.
5. *Example*: A tech reviewer might tweet quick tips, share unboxing videos, and post threads analyzing the latest gadgets.

3.5 Engaging with Your Audience

1. **Active** **Interaction**
Respond to comments, mentions, and DMs to show that you value your followers.
2. **Participate** **in** **Conversations**
Join discussions relevant to your niche. Use **Twitter Spaces** to share insights in live audio sessions.
3. **Show** **Appreciation**
Thank your audience for their support, whether by acknowledging their comments, reposting user-generated content, or celebrating milestones like follower counts.
Example: A creator might tweet, "Thank you for helping me reach 10K followers! Grateful for all your support ."

3.6 Leveraging Hashtags and Trends

1. **Use** **Relevant** **Hashtags**
Incorporate niche-specific and trending hashtags to increase your content's visibility.
Example: A food blogger might use #Foodie, #HomeCooking, or #RecipeOfTheDay.
2. **Stay** **Updated** **on** **Trends**
Monitor trending topics and participate when relevant. This can help position you as an active and engaged creator.

3.7 Collaborating with Others

1. **Network** **with** **Influencers**
   Collaborations with influencers in your niche can help you tap into their audience. *Example*: A fitness influencer might partner with a nutritionist for joint content.
2. **Guest** **Contributions**
   Offer to write guest posts, appear on podcasts, or participate in Twitter Spaces hosted by others. This expands your reach.

3.8 Monitoring and Adjusting Your Strategy

1. **Analytics**
   Regularly review performance metrics, such as engagement rates, follower growth, and impressions. Use X's built-in analytics to understand what works best.
2. **Feedback**
   Pay attention to audience feedback to refine your content strategy.
3. **Continuous** **Improvement**
   Stay flexible and adapt to new trends, audience preferences, and platform updates.

Conclusion

Building a strong personal brand on X requires intentionality, consistency, and authenticity. By defining your identity, creating engaging content, and actively engaging with your audience, you can establish a compelling presence that attracts followers and opens up monetization opportunities. In the next chapter, we'll explore X's monetization features in detail, helping you turn your personal brand into a source of revenue.

Chapter 4: Building and Engaging Your Audience on X

Establishing a robust and engaged audience is a cornerstone of success on X. A loyal community not only amplifies your reach but also forms the foundation for monetization. This chapter provides actionable strategies to attract followers, foster engagement, and cultivate a thriving community that values your content.

4.1 Crafting a Compelling Profile

Your profile is your first opportunity to capture the interest of potential followers. A well-designed profile reflects your brand and encourages users to hit the "Follow" button.

1. **Profile Picture**
    - Use a high-quality image that is visually appealing and professional.
    - For individuals, a clear headshot works best. For brands, use a recognizable logo.
2. *Example*: A personal development coach might use a smiling, approachable headshot, while a bakery could feature its logo or an enticing image of its best-selling pastry.
3. **Bio**
    - Write a concise and informative bio that highlights your niche, expertise, and personality.
    - Include a call-to-action (CTA), like "Follow for daily tips" or "DM for inquiries."
4. *Example*: "Marketing Strategist | Helping small businesses grow online | DM for consultations."
5. **Header Image**
    - Select a header that visually complements your profile and reinforces your brand identity.
    - Use this space to showcase achievements, promote products, or display your tagline.
6. *Example*: A travel influencer might use a panoramic shot of a destination they've visited, while a tech brand could highlight its latest product launch.

4.2 Consistent and Valuable Content

Consistency and value are the keys to growing your audience. Providing meaningful content ensures followers keep coming back.

1. **Content Calendar**
    - Plan your posts using tools like **Hootsuite** or **Notion** to maintain a regular posting schedule.

- Post during peak times when your audience is most active.
2. **Value-Driven Posts**
   - Share content that educates, entertains, or inspires your followers.
   - Offer actionable insights, step-by-step guides, or exclusive updates in your niche.
3. *Example*: A fitness coach might share workout routines, while a tech expert could post software tutorials.
4. **Multimedia Integration**
   - Use images, videos, GIFs, and infographics to make your posts visually appealing and engaging.
   - Keep multimedia content high-quality and relevant to your message.
5. *Example*: A chef might share recipe videos, while an artist could post time-lapse recordings of their creative process.

4.3 Leveraging Hashtags and Trends

Hashtags and trends help expand your reach by making your content discoverable to a broader audience.

1. **Relevant Hashtags**
   - Research hashtags relevant to your niche. Tools like **Hashtagify** can help identify popular hashtags.
   - Use a mix of popular and niche-specific hashtags to balance visibility and target relevance.
2. *Example*: A fashion blogger might use #OOTD (Outfit of the Day) alongside a niche tag like #SustainableFashion.
3. **Trending Topics**
   - Monitor trending topics on X's homepage and participate when they align with your brand.
   - Add your unique perspective to trending conversations to showcase expertise and relevance.
4. *Example*: During a major tech conference, a tech influencer could tweet insights about announcements and innovations.

4.4 Engaging with Your Audience

Engagement is the foundation of community building. Active interaction shows your followers that you value their time and input.

1. **Respond to Interactions**
   - Reply to comments, mentions, and direct messages promptly.
   - Use responses to spark conversations or clarify questions.
2. *Example*: If someone asks for advice on a tweet, respond with additional tips or helpful resources.
3. **Encourage Participation**

- Ask open-ended questions or create polls to involve your audience.
- Example questions: "What's the best advice you've received?" or "Which of these designs do you prefer?"
4. **Acknowledge Mentions**
   - Thank users who share your content or mention you in a positive light.
   - Retweet user-generated content to show appreciation and build goodwill.

4.5 Collaborations and Networking

Collaborations expand your reach by introducing you to new audiences and providing mutual benefits.

1. **Identify Potential Partners**
   - Look for creators or brands with similar or complementary audiences.
   - Approach collaborators with a clear idea of the value you bring to the partnership.
2. **Collaborative Content**
   - Co-create threads, videos, or live discussions to provide diverse perspectives and value.
   - Example: A health coach and a nutritionist could collaborate on a thread about balanced diets and exercise routines.
3. **Cross-Promotion**
   - Share each other's content to increase visibility.
   - Example: Two podcasters in the same niche might promote each other's episodes.

4.6 Analyzing Performance

Regular analysis helps you understand what works, what doesn't, and how to optimize your strategy.

1. **Analytics Tools**
   - Use X's native analytics to monitor metrics such as impressions, engagement rates, and follower growth.
   - Third-party tools like **Sprout Social** or **Buffer Analytics** can provide deeper insights.
2. **Content Evaluation**
   - Identify high-performing posts and analyze why they succeeded.
   - Look at factors such as timing, format, and audience interaction.
3. **Adjust Strategies**
   - Based on analytical insights, refine your content and engagement strategies.
   - For instance, if videos outperform text-based tweets, focus more on video content.

4.7 Adhering to X's Guidelines

Maintaining compliance with X's policies ensures a safe and positive environment for you and your audience.

1. **Content Standards**
   - Familiarize yourself with X's content guidelines to avoid violations like spam, hate speech, or copyright infringement.
2. **Community Engagement**
   - Promote respectful interactions within your community.
   - Set clear boundaries for acceptable behavior and address inappropriate comments promptly.

Conclusion

Building and engaging your audience on X takes time, effort, and consistency. By crafting a compelling profile, creating valuable content, fostering meaningful interactions, and analyzing your performance, you can cultivate a loyal and active community. This engaged audience not only amplifies your content but also lays the groundwork for successful monetization. In the next chapter, we'll explore best practices for leveraging X's monetization features to turn your audience into a sustainable income stream.

Chapter 5: Monetization Strategies on X

Monetizing your presence on X requires a strategic approach that leverages the platform's unique features while aligning with your content and audience. From creator subscriptions to affiliate marketing, X offers diverse ways to turn your engagement into income. This chapter explores these monetization avenues in depth, providing actionable guidance to help you maximize your earning potential.

5.1 Creator Subscriptions

Creator Subscriptions allow you to offer exclusive, premium content to subscribers for a monthly fee. This model helps you foster a community of dedicated followers while generating a steady income stream.

Eligibility Requirements

To enable Creator Subscriptions, you must meet the following criteria:

- Be at least 18 years old.
- Have a minimum of **500 followers**.
- Have posted at least **25 times in the last 30 days**.
- Reside in a country where X's monetization programs are available.

Setting Up Creator Subscriptions

1. Navigate to the **Monetization** section in your account settings.
2. Complete the application process, including identity verification and linking a verified **Stripe** account for payouts.
3. Set your subscription pricing at one of X's tiers: $2.99, $4.99, or $9.99 per month.

Best Practices

- Offer exclusive content like behind-the-scenes updates, tutorials, or personalized shoutouts.
- Regularly promote your subscription service through posts and direct engagement.
- Deliver on promises to retain subscribers and encourage positive word-of-mouth.

Example: A graphic designer might offer tutorials and design templates exclusively for subscribers, while a fitness coach could provide customized workout plans and live Q&A sessions.

5.2 Ads Revenue Sharing

X's **Ads Revenue Sharing** program rewards creators by sharing ad revenue generated from ads displayed in replies to their posts.

Eligibility Requirements

To qualify for Ads Revenue Sharing, you must:

- Subscribe to **X Premium** or **Verified Organizations**.
- Accumulate at least **15 million impressions** on your posts in the last three months.
- Have at least **500 followers**.

Application Process

1. Go to the **Monetization** section in your account settings.
2. Apply for the program and complete verification steps.
3. Connect a verified **Stripe** account to receive payouts.

Maximizing Earnings

- Create engaging content that sparks replies and discussions, increasing the likelihood of ads being displayed.
- Maintain a consistent posting schedule to grow impressions over time.
- Foster a sense of community by engaging with followers through replies and comments.

Example: A tech reviewer might post a thread about the latest gadgets, encouraging users to discuss and share opinions, thereby boosting impressions and ad revenue.

5.3 Tips and Donations

The **Tips** feature enables followers to support creators directly as a token of appreciation for their content.

Setting Up Tips

1. Enable the **Tips** feature in your account settings.
2. Connect a payment processor, such as **PayPal**, **Venmo**, or **Cash App**, to receive funds.

Encouraging Tips

- Let your audience know about the tipping option through posts or your profile bio.
- Show appreciation by thanking those who tip and giving shoutouts to enhance engagement.

Example: A writer sharing free poetry might thank tippers by offering a personalized message or access to exclusive poems.

5.4 Affiliate Marketing

Affiliate marketing involves promoting products or services and earning commissions for sales or leads generated through your referral links.

Implementing Affiliate Marketing

1. Join affiliate programs relevant to your niche, such as Amazon Associates or specialized programs in your industry.
2. Share affiliate links in your posts, ensuring they provide value to your followers.
3. Transparently disclose your affiliate relationships to maintain audience trust.

Best Practices

- Promote products you genuinely use or believe in.
- Create engaging content like reviews, tutorials, or recommendations to showcase the product's benefits.
- Monitor performance metrics to focus on high-performing affiliate partnerships.

Example: A beauty influencer might review skincare products, including affiliate links for followers to purchase them.

5.5 Sponsored Content and Brand Partnerships

Collaborating with brands for sponsored posts or partnerships can be a lucrative way to monetize your presence on X.

Approaching Brands

- Develop a **media kit** highlighting your audience demographics, engagement rates, and examples of your best-performing content.
- Reach out to brands that align with your niche, proposing specific collaboration ideas.

Creating Sponsored Content

- Clearly disclose sponsored posts to comply with advertising regulations.
- Integrate brand messaging seamlessly into your content to maintain authenticity.
- Maintain creative control to ensure the sponsored content resonates with your audience.

Example: A travel blogger might partner with a luggage brand to showcase its products during a trip, blending personal storytelling with promotional content.

5.6 Selling Products or Services

Leverage your presence on X to promote and sell your own products or services, turning followers into customers.

Strategies

- Share links to your store or services in posts and your profile bio.
- Offer exclusive promotions or discounts to your X followers.
- Highlight customer testimonials or success stories to build credibility.

Best Practices

- Ensure your offerings align with your audience's interests and needs.
- Provide exceptional customer service to foster loyalty and encourage repeat business.
- Continuously gather and act on feedback to improve your offerings.

Example: A course creator might use X to promote online classes, sharing success stories from past students to attract new enrollments.

5.7 Crowdfunding and Membership Platforms

Crowdfunding platforms like **Patreon** or **Ko-fi** allow creators to receive ongoing support from their audience in exchange for exclusive perks.

Implementing Crowdfunding

1. Set up a profile on a platform like Patreon or Ko-fi.
2. Define support tiers with clear rewards, such as exclusive content, early access, or personalized shoutouts.
3. Promote your crowdfunding page through your X profile and posts.

Best Practices

- Offer valuable, exclusive content to incentivize support.
- Engage regularly with your supporters, making them feel appreciated and involved.
- Consistently deliver on promised rewards to maintain trust and loyalty.

Example: A musician might share unreleased tracks or behind-the-scenes videos with Patreon supporters, fostering a closer connection with their most loyal fans.

Conclusion

X provides a variety of monetization opportunities, from subscriptions and ad revenue sharing to affiliate marketing and brand partnerships. By strategically implementing these methods and aligning them with your audience's needs, you can turn your presence on X into a sustainable source of income. In the next chapter, we'll explore how to measure and analyze your performance on X to continuously refine your strategies and maximize your success.

Chapter 6: Monetization Strategies on X

Monetizing your presence on X requires a well-thought-out strategy that takes full advantage of the platform's features while aligning with your content and audience. This chapter explores the monetization avenues available on X and provides practical guidance on implementing them to maximize your earning potential.

6.1 X Premium Subscriptions

X offers a tiered subscription model—**Basic**, **Premium**, and **Premium+**—designed to cater to different user needs while offering creators unique monetization opportunities.

Basic Tier

- **Price**: $3 per month or $32 per year.
- **Features**:
  - Ability to edit posts within 30 minutes.
  - Write long-form posts up to **25,000 characters**.
  - Upload videos up to **three hours** long.
  - Organizational tools like **bookmark folders** and **reader mode** for threads.
- **Who Should Use It**: This tier is ideal for creators who want basic enhancements for content creation and organization without advanced monetization tools.

Premium Tier

- **Price**: $8 per month or $84 per year.
- **Features**:
  - Includes all Basic features.
  - Earn a share of ad revenue based on engagement.
  - Access to **Media Studio** and **X Pro** for professional content management.
  - Set up **creator subscriptions** to monetize exclusive content.
  - Reduced ads (50% fewer than Basic users).
  - Verified checkmark for account credibility.
- **Who Should Use It**: This tier is best for creators aiming to monetize through ads, subscriptions, or advanced content tools.

Premium+ Tier

- **Price**: $16 per month or $168 per year.
- **Features**:
  - All Premium features included.
  - **Ad-free experience**.
  - Ability to post articles with advanced formatting.
  - Highest prioritization in replies, increasing visibility.

- **Who Should Use It**: Ideal for high-profile creators and brands prioritizing visibility and an enhanced, ad-free experience.

6.2 Creator Subscriptions

Creator Subscriptions allow you to offer exclusive, paid content to subscribers. This fosters a community of loyal supporters while generating a steady income stream.

How to Activate

1. Navigate to the **X Premium** section on the sidebar.
2. Select **Monetization** and then click **Subscriptions**.
3. Set up your subscription pricing, and ensure that your payout account is linked to **Stripe**.
4. Withdraw earnings once you reach a $50 threshold.

Best Practices

- Provide exclusive content such as behind-the-scenes insights, tutorials, or personalized Q&A sessions.
- Promote your subscription offering through posts and direct engagement with your audience.
- Consistently deliver high-value content to retain subscribers.

Example: A cooking influencer might offer subscribers exclusive recipes, live cooking demos, or early access to new videos.

6.3 Ad Revenue Sharing

X's **ad revenue-sharing program** rewards creators for engagement from Premium users on their content.

How It Works

- Premium users see fewer ads, but ads that are displayed generate revenue shared with creators.
- The more engagement (likes, replies, reposts) you receive from Premium users, the higher your earnings.

Maximizing Earnings

- Focus on creating engaging content that resonates with Premium users.
- Use storytelling, humor, or thought-provoking questions to spark replies and interactions.
- Maintain a consistent posting schedule to increase impressions over time.

Example: A tech blogger who posts threads analyzing the latest gadgets could encourage detailed discussions in replies, driving higher engagement from Premium users.

6.4 Affiliate Marketing

Affiliate marketing is a straightforward way to earn commissions by promoting products or services that align with your audience's interests.

How to Get Started

1. Join affiliate programs such as **Amazon Associates**, **ShareASale**, or industry-specific networks.
2. Share affiliate links in your posts, ensuring they naturally fit your content.
3. Disclose affiliate relationships to maintain transparency and audience trust.

Best Practices

- Promote products or services you genuinely believe in to preserve authenticity.
- Create content that naturally integrates affiliate links, such as tutorials, reviews, or recommendations.
- Monitor your affiliate performance to identify successful campaigns and refine your approach.

Example: A fitness creator might review workout equipment and include affiliate links for followers to purchase them.

6.5 Sponsored Content

Collaborating with brands for sponsored posts is one of the most lucrative monetization strategies.

How to Approach Brands

- Develop a **media kit** showcasing your audience demographics, engagement metrics, and best-performing content.
- Identify brands that align with your niche and propose mutually beneficial partnerships.
- Negotiate terms covering compensation, content expectations, and disclosure requirements.

Creating Effective Sponsored Content

- Ensure sponsored posts are **clearly disclosed** to comply with advertising regulations.

- Blend the brand's message seamlessly into your content to maintain authenticity.
- Retain creative control to ensure the content aligns with your personal brand.

Example: A travel influencer might partner with a hotel chain, sharing posts about their stay while highlighting the hotel's amenities.

6.6 Selling Products or Services

Your presence on X can serve as a powerful marketing tool for promoting and selling your own offerings.

Examples of What to Sell

- **Merchandise**: Branded clothing, mugs, or other items.
- **Digital Products**: E-books, templates, or online courses.
- **Services**: Consulting, coaching, or freelance work.

Best Practices

- Share links to your offerings in your bio or posts.
- Offer exclusive promotions or discounts to your X followers.
- Use testimonials or success stories to build credibility.

Example: A graphic designer might sell design templates for social media, offering discounts for followers who purchase directly from their X profile.

6.7 Best Practices for Monetization

To succeed in monetizing your presence on X, follow these essential practices:

1. **Content** **Quality**
   Consistently create high-quality, engaging content that provides value to your audience. This builds trust and encourages loyalty.
2. **Audience** **Engagement**
   Actively interact with your followers by replying to comments, asking questions, and fostering discussions.
3. **Transparency**
   Clearly disclose any sponsored content, affiliate links, or partnerships to maintain credibility and comply with advertising regulations.
4. **Compliance**
   Adhere to X's monetization policies and guidelines to avoid penalties or account suspension. Stay informed about changes to these policies.

Conclusion

X provides diverse monetization options tailored to creators with varying goals and niches. By strategically utilizing tools like Premium Subscriptions, ad revenue sharing, affiliate marketing, and brand partnerships, you can effectively generate income while maintaining audience trust and engagement. In the next chapter, we'll explore how to analyze performance and leverage data to optimize your monetization strategy.

Chapter 7: Leveraging Analytics to Optimize Your X Strategy

Understanding and utilizing analytics is essential for fine-tuning your content strategy, maximizing engagement, and achieving your goals on X. Analytics provide insights into what works, what doesn't, and how your audience interacts with your content. This chapter delves into the tools and techniques for tracking performance, interpreting data, and making data-driven decisions to enhance your presence on the platform.

7.1 Accessing X Analytics

X provides a built-in analytics dashboard that gives you a clear overview of your account's performance. This tool is a powerful resource for understanding how your content resonates with your audience.

Navigating to Analytics

1. Click on your **profile icon** in the top-right corner of the homepage.
2. Select **Analytics** from the dropdown menu to access the dashboard.

Overview of Analytics Dashboard

The dashboard is divided into several tabs that provide detailed insights:

- **Home Tab**: Displays a 28-day summary of key metrics, including:
    - **Tweet Impressions**: Total views of your tweets.
    - **Profile Visits**: The number of times users viewed your profile.
    - **Mentions**: The number of times other users mentioned your handle.
    - **Follower Growth**: Tracks the net gain or loss of followers.
- **Tweets Tab**: Breaks down performance for individual tweets, including:
    - **Impressions**.
    - **Engagements** (likes, replies, retweets, clicks).
    - **Engagement Rate** (engagements as a percentage of impressions).
- **Audience Tab**: Provides demographic and interest-based insights, including:
    - Follower **locations**.
    - Top **interests** of your audience.
    - **Gender and age** breakdowns.

7.2 Key Metrics to Monitor

Certain metrics are particularly important for evaluating your content strategy and audience engagement.

Impressions

- Reflects how many times your tweets were displayed to users.
- A high number of impressions indicates your content is reaching a wide audience.

Engagements

- Includes actions such as likes, retweets, replies, link clicks, and profile clicks.
- High engagement suggests your content resonates with your audience.

Engagement Rate

- **Formula**: (Engagements ÷ Impressions) × 100.
- A high engagement rate indicates your content is not only seen but also actively interacted with by your audience.

Follower Growth

- Tracks changes in your follower count over time.
- A steady increase in followers signifies your content is appealing and attracting new users.

Example: If your engagement rate for posts with polls is consistently higher than that for static images, you might prioritize using more interactive content in your strategy.

7.3 Utilizing Third-Party Analytics Tools

While X's native analytics provide excellent insights, third-party tools can offer additional features for in-depth analysis and strategic planning.

Popular Tools

1. **Hootsuite**
   - Tracks audience engagement.
   - Identifies optimal posting times.
   - Provides comparisons of content performance.
2. **Sprout Social**
   - Offers detailed reporting on audience growth and engagement trends.
   - Includes competitor analysis to benchmark your performance.
3. **Buffer**
   - Analyzes post performance.
   - Provides actionable suggestions for improving future content.

Example: Use Hootsuite to schedule posts at peak times identified by X analytics, ensuring maximum visibility for your content.

7.4 Interpreting Data to Refine Your Strategy

Analyzing your analytics data helps you make informed decisions to optimize your content and engagement efforts.

Identify Top-Performing Content

- Examine tweets with the highest engagement and impressions.
- Determine what made them successful—timing, tone, format, or topic—and replicate these factors in future posts.

Understand Audience Preferences

- Use demographic and interest data to tailor your content to your followers' preferences.
- Example: If your audience is primarily interested in technology and finance, focus on creating content around those topics.

Optimize Posting Times

- Identify when your audience is most active by tracking engagement patterns.
- Schedule posts during these times to increase visibility and interaction.

Monitor Engagement Patterns

- Compare how different content types perform (e.g., videos, images, polls, threads).
- Adjust your strategy to include more of the formats that generate the most engagement.

Example: If polls receive significantly higher engagement than standard tweets, incorporate more polls into your weekly content plan.

7.5 Setting Goals and Measuring Success

Clear, measurable goals are essential for tracking your progress and staying motivated.

Define Specific Goals

Set objectives that are both realistic and measurable:

- Increase engagement rate by 10% over the next month.
- Gain 500 new followers within three months.
- Achieve 50,000 tweet impressions in a 28-day period.

Regularly Review Progress

- Use analytics to monitor your performance against these goals.
- Adjust your strategy as needed based on what the data reveals.

Celebrate Milestones

- Acknowledge your achievements to stay motivated and maintain momentum.
- Example: Share a thank-you tweet when you reach a significant milestone, like gaining 10,000 followers.

Conclusion

Leveraging analytics effectively allows you to refine your strategy, better understand your audience, and maximize your presence on X. By monitoring key metrics, utilizing third-party tools, and setting actionable goals, you can continuously optimize your content for engagement and growth. In the next chapter, we'll explore advanced tactics for growing and sustaining your community on X to further boost your monetization potential.

Chapter 8: Navigating X's Policies and Guidelines

Understanding and adhering to X's policies and guidelines is vital for maintaining a positive presence on the platform. Compliance ensures that your content aligns with community standards, protects your eligibility for monetization, and minimizes the risk of account penalties. This chapter provides an overview of X's key policies and practical advice on how to stay within the rules.

8.1 Content Guidelines

X has specific rules governing the type of content that can be shared. Adhering to these guidelines is essential for protecting your account and ensuring a safe, respectful environment.

Prohibited Content

X strictly prohibits content that:

- Promotes **hate speech** or **harassment**.
- Contains **threats**, incites violence, or glorifies illegal activities.
- Spreads **false information** that could harm public safety or wellbeing.

Example: A tweet encouraging violence or bullying another user could result in immediate action, such as removal or account suspension.

Sensitive Media

X allows certain types of sensitive content but requires it to be properly labeled:

- **Adult Content**: As of June 2024, X permits consensual adult content as long as it is clearly labeled and adheres to legal and ethical standards.
- **Violent or Graphic Media**: Such content must include warning labels to prevent it from being shown automatically.

Tip: Creators should use X's built-in tools to mark sensitive posts appropriately. Failure to label sensitive media can lead to content removal or account penalties.

8.2 Monetization Policies

Participating in X's monetization programs requires strict adherence to both general and program-specific rules.

Eligibility Requirements

To qualify for monetization, creators must typically meet:

- **Follower and engagement thresholds** (e.g., 500 followers or 15 million impressions over three months for ad revenue sharing).
- Full compliance with X's **content guidelines**.

Program-Specific Policies

Each monetization feature has unique criteria:

- **Ad Revenue Sharing**: Content must generate meaningful engagement from X Premium users to qualify for earnings.
- **Subscriptions**: Exclusive content provided to subscribers must comply with general platform rules and avoid restricted categories.

Tip: Regularly check X's monetization guidelines to ensure your account and content meet current eligibility criteria.

8.3 Community Standards

Building a positive and respectful community on X is not just good practice—it's also essential for maintaining your account's standing.

Interaction Guidelines

- Promote **constructive conversations** by responding respectfully, even to criticism.
- Avoid participating in or amplifying **harassment**, **abusive language**, or **toxicity**.

Example: If a heated discussion arises in your replies, focus on de-escalating tensions or reporting inappropriate behavior rather than engaging in conflicts.

Reporting Mechanisms

X provides tools to report violations of its community standards:

- Report abusive users or content directly from tweets.
- Block or mute accounts that engage in harmful behavior.

Tip: Actively maintaining a respectful community improves your audience's experience and helps protect your reputation.

8.4 Compliance and Enforcement

Non-compliance with X's policies can result in various consequences, ranging from content removal to account suspension or permanent bans.

Account Actions

Violations of X's guidelines may lead to:

- **Warnings**: Minor infractions may result in warning messages from X.
- **Temporary Suspensions**: Repeat offenses or serious violations may lead to restricted access.
- **Permanent Bans**: Severe or repeated violations can result in the loss of your account.

Example: Consistently sharing misinformation or unmarked sensitive media could escalate from warnings to permanent suspension.

Content Removal

Inappropriate content may be removed without notice. If this happens repeatedly, it can negatively affect your account's standing, reducing visibility and monetization eligibility.

8.5 Staying Informed

X's policies are subject to change as the platform evolves. Staying up-to-date with these changes is crucial for compliance.

Regular Updates

- Periodically review X's official **policy pages** to stay informed about updates to content or monetization guidelines.
- Follow X's **official accounts** for announcements regarding policy changes.

Community Resources

- Use X's **support channels** to seek clarification on policies or report issues.
- Engage with **community forums** where other creators share experiences and insights about navigating the platform's guidelines.

Example: A creator might join a discussion in a digital marketing forum to better understand how X enforces specific monetization policies.

Conclusion

Adhering to X's policies and guidelines is crucial for maintaining a positive presence and ensuring continued eligibility for monetization. By staying informed about the platform's rules, fostering respectful community interactions, and complying with content standards, you can safeguard your account and build trust with your audience. In the next chapter, we'll explore advanced techniques for analyzing and refining your performance on X to further optimize your content and engagement strategies.

Chapter 9: Leveraging X's Features for Audience Engagement

Effectively utilizing X's diverse features can transform passive followers into an active, engaged community. By strategically employing tools such as X Spaces, polls, multimedia content, and trending topics, you can foster meaningful interactions, boost visibility, and build lasting relationships with your audience. This chapter explores key features and strategies to maximize your engagement on the platform.

9.1 Utilizing X Spaces

X Spaces provides a live audio platform for real-time conversations with your audience, making it an excellent tool for fostering direct engagement.

Hosting Spaces

- **Topic Selection**: Choose topics that align with your audience's interests and expertise.
  Example: A personal finance coach might host a Space on "Saving Strategies for 2024."
- **Scheduling**: Announce your Space in advance and provide reminders through posts to maximize attendance.
- **Moderation**: Designate co-hosts or moderators to manage discussions, ensuring a respectful and productive environment.

Benefits

- **Direct Interaction**: Spaces allow for real-time Q&A sessions, creating a stronger sense of connection with your audience.
- **In-Depth Discussions**: The live format enables more nuanced conversations than text-based posts.

Example: A tech influencer could host a Space after a major product launch to discuss its features and answer audience questions.

9.2 Engaging with Polls

Polls are an interactive feature that encourages participation and provides valuable audience insights.

Creating Polls

- **Relevance**: Choose topics that reflect your audience's interests or preferences. *Example*: A food blogger might ask, "What type of recipes should I share next? Options: Desserts, Quick Meals, Healthy Snacks."
- **Clarity**: Use simple language and concise answer options to ensure accessibility.

Benefits

- **Encourages Interaction**: Polls invite followers to engage, even if they don't usually comment or reply.
- **Audience Insights**: Results can help you tailor your content strategy based on audience preferences.

Example: A fitness trainer could use polls to decide the focus of their next video, such as "Strength Training" or "Yoga for Beginners."

9.3 Sharing Multimedia Content

Incorporating images, videos, and GIFs into your posts can significantly boost engagement. Visual content is more likely to catch the eye and encourage interaction.

Best Practices

- **Quality**: Use high-resolution visuals that are relevant to your content and visually appealing. *Example*: A travel influencer might share stunning destination photos with captions detailing their experiences.
- **Accessibility**: Include alt text or descriptions for images to ensure inclusivity for visually impaired users.

Benefits

- **Enhanced Visual Appeal**: Multimedia content stands out on the timeline, increasing the likelihood of interaction.
- **Effective Storytelling**: Videos and images can convey complex ideas quickly and memorably.

Example: A digital marketer might share a video walkthrough of setting up an ad campaign, making the process more relatable and engaging.

9.4 Participating in Trending Topics

Engaging with trending topics allows you to tap into larger conversations and expand your reach to new audiences.

Strategies

- **Relevance**: Focus on trends that align with your brand's niche and audience interests.
  Example: A tech blogger might join a conversation about a major tech conference or product release.
- **Timeliness**: Act quickly to capitalize on the momentum of a trend.

Benefits

- **Increased Visibility**: Trending topics often attract more views and interactions, exposing your content to a broader audience.
- **Demonstrates Awareness**: Engaging with current events and trends shows your brand's relevance and attentiveness.

Example: A nonprofit organization might participate in trending topics around global charity initiatives, using hashtags to amplify their message.

9.5 Collaborating with Other Users

Collaborations introduce your content to new audiences and build stronger connections within your niche.

Approaches

- **Joint Spaces**: Co-host live audio discussions with other creators on shared topics.
  Example: A fitness coach and a nutritionist might co-host a Space about "Healthy Habits for the New Year."
- **Content Sharing**: Retweet, comment on, or tag other creators' posts to build rapport and encourage mutual promotion.

Benefits

- **Broadened Reach**: Collaborating exposes your content to another creator's audience.
- **Community Building**: Partnerships foster a sense of collaboration and mutual support within your niche.

Example: A lifestyle blogger might partner with a fashion influencer to cross-promote each other's content during a seasonal campaign.

9.6 Engaging Through Direct Messages

Direct messages (DMs) provide a more personal way to connect with your audience, offering opportunities for deeper engagement.

Best Practices

- **Responsiveness**: Reply to messages promptly and thoughtfully.
- **Professionalism**: Maintain a respectful and courteous tone, even in informal conversations.

Benefits

- **Builds Trust**: Personalized communication strengthens relationships and fosters loyalty.
- **Feedback Opportunities**: DMs allow followers to share insights or ask questions they may not feel comfortable posting publicly.

Example: A creator might use DMs to thank followers for their support or to clarify a query about their content.

Conclusion

By strategically leveraging X's features, you can significantly enhance audience engagement and create a vibrant, interactive community. Whether hosting live Spaces, creating polls, or collaborating with other creators, these tools provide a dynamic platform to strengthen connections with your audience. In the next chapter, we'll explore strategies for scaling your efforts and sustaining growth on X, ensuring long-term success.

Chapter 10: Collaborating with Influencers and Brands on X

Strategic collaborations with influencers and brands on X can dramatically enhance your reach, credibility, and audience engagement. By partnering with individuals and organizations whose values and audience align with yours, you can create mutually beneficial content that resonates with followers and strengthens your brand. This chapter outlines actionable strategies for identifying, initiating, and managing collaborations effectively.

10.1 Identifying Potential Partners

Selecting the right partners is the foundation of a successful collaboration.

Relevance

- Look for influencers or brands whose content aligns with your niche and audience interests.
- Ensure that their values and messaging complement your brand to maintain authenticity.

Example: A fitness coach might collaborate with a health supplement brand or a lifestyle influencer who promotes wellness.

Engagement Metrics

- Focus on partners with high engagement rates rather than simply a large follower count.
- Assess the quality of their content, their followers' demographics, and how actively their audience interacts with their posts.

Tip: Tools like **HypeAuditor** or **Social Blade** can help you evaluate potential partners' engagement rates and audience authenticity.

10.2 Approaching Influencers and Brands

A thoughtful approach increases the likelihood of securing collaborations.

Personalized Outreach

- Craft individualized messages that demonstrate your familiarity with their content and values.
- Highlight specific reasons why you think a collaboration would be beneficial.

Example:

"Hi [Name], I'm a big fan of your posts about [specific topic]. I think our shared focus on [common interest] could make for an exciting collaboration. Would you be interested in co-hosting a Space or creating a joint thread about [topic]?"

Value Proposition

- Clearly articulate how the partnership will benefit both parties.
- Emphasize the value you can provide to their audience, such as increasing visibility, expanding their reach, or offering unique content.

Tip: Position the partnership as a win-win by showing how it aligns with both of your goals.

10.3 Structuring Collaborations

A well-structured collaboration ensures clarity, value, and a seamless experience for both parties.

Content Co-Creation

- Create joint content that showcases both brands authentically, such as:
  - Co-authored posts or threads.
  - Live discussions using **X Spaces**.
  - Exclusive offers or giveaways for followers of both parties.

Example: A tech reviewer and a gadget brand could co-create a product demo thread, combining the creator's audience reach with the brand's expertise.

Cross-Promotion

- Share each other's content on your profiles, tagging each other to ensure visibility.
- Keep the promotion organic and authentic to avoid alienating audiences.

Example: A travel blogger and a hotel chain might collaborate by sharing photos and reviews, tagging each other in posts to attract mutual followers.

10.4 Maintaining Authenticity

Authenticity is key to building trust with your audience during collaborations.

Transparency

- Always disclose partnerships in line with X's guidelines and advertising standards.
- Use clear labels like #Sponsored or #Ad to ensure your audience understands the nature of the collaboration.

Consistency

- Ensure that the tone and style of collaborative content align with your brand's voice and values.
- Avoid promoting products or services that don't fit your niche, even if they offer lucrative deals.

Example: A sustainable fashion influencer should collaborate only with brands that prioritize ethical practices to maintain credibility with their audience.

10.5 Measuring Collaboration Success

Tracking and analyzing results helps you evaluate the effectiveness of your collaborations and refine future strategies.

Analytics Monitoring

- Track performance indicators such as:
    - **Engagement Rates**: Likes, comments, retweets, and replies on collaborative posts.
    - **Follower Growth**: New followers gained during or after the collaboration.
    - **Conversion Metrics**: Click-through rates or sales generated from promotional content.

Tip: Use X's built-in analytics or tools like **Google Analytics** and **Bitly** for tracking links.

Feedback Collection

- Ask your audience for feedback on the collaboration to gauge their perception and interest.
- Use polls, comments, or DMs to gather insights on what they enjoyed or would like to see next.

Example: After a giveaway collaboration, ask participants what they thought about the process and the prize.

Conclusion

Collaborating with influencers and brands on X is a powerful strategy for expanding your reach, boosting credibility, and delivering greater value to your audience. By identifying relevant partners, crafting authentic content, and measuring success thoughtfully, you can build long-term partnerships that drive growth and engagement. In the next chapter, we'll explore strategies for staying adaptable and evolving your presence on X in response to emerging trends and platform changes.

Chapter 11: Managing and Growing Your Community on X

Cultivating a vibrant and engaged community on X is essential for achieving long-term growth, maintaining an active presence, and monetizing effectively. A well-nurtured community not only supports your goals but also creates a space where members feel valued and connected. This chapter provides actionable strategies to build, manage, and expand your community on X while fostering meaningful interactions.

11.1 Establishing a Welcoming Environment

Creating an inviting and respectful space is foundational to building a strong community.

Set Clear Guidelines

- Develop and share community standards that outline acceptable behavior.
- Use pinned tweets or your bio to communicate these guidelines clearly.

Example: "Welcome to my X community! Let's keep discussions respectful and engaging. Harassment and spam will not be tolerated."

Encourage Inclusivity

- Foster an environment where diverse perspectives are welcomed and valued.
- Encourage members to share their opinions and experiences openly, as long as they adhere to community guidelines.

Tip: Acknowledge diverse viewpoints by retweeting or engaging with thoughtful, constructive replies.

11.2 Consistent Engagement

Consistent interaction with your audience is key to sustaining an active community.

Regular Interaction

- Respond promptly to comments, mentions, and DMs to show appreciation and build relationships.
- Engage authentically, adding value to conversations rather than posting generic replies.

Example: Instead of replying "Thanks!" to a comment, add depth: "Thank you! I'm glad this tip helped—let me know if you'd like more insights on this topic!"

Host Interactive Sessions

- Use features like **X Spaces** to host live discussions, workshops, or Q&A sessions.
- Announce sessions in advance and encourage audience participation with specific questions or topics.

Example: A travel blogger might host a Space on "Best Budget Destinations for 2024" and invite followers to share their own experiences.

11.3 Providing Value-Driven Content

Content that addresses your audience's interests and needs strengthens their connection to your community.

Educational Posts

- Share tips, tutorials, or step-by-step guides tailored to your niche.
- Break down complex topics into easily digestible posts or threads.

Example: A personal finance expert might post a thread on "5 Simple Steps to Create a Monthly Budget" with actionable tips.

Exclusive Offers

- Provide special deals, early access, or members-only content as a way to reward your community's loyalty.
- Example: Offer discount codes for your products or services exclusively to followers who engage with your posts.

11.4 Recognizing and Rewarding Members

Acknowledging and rewarding active members strengthens their sense of belonging and encourages continued participation.

Highlight Contributions

- Feature user-generated content, reply to insightful comments, or give shout-outs to active members.

Example: "A big shout-out to @User123 for their fantastic idea in yesterday's poll! Your input is always appreciated."

Implement Reward Systems

- Introduce incentives like badges, exclusive access, or discounts for members who actively participate.
- Gamify engagement by recognizing milestones such as "Top Contributor of the Month."

Tip: If you have a monetization program, consider offering a free month of subscriptions to your most loyal followers.

11.5 Facilitating Member Connections

Encouraging connections among community members fosters a sense of unity and shared purpose.

Create Sub-Groups

- Develop smaller communities within your broader audience, focusing on niche topics.
- Use hashtags or dedicated threads to organize discussions.

Example: A tech influencer could create a #GadgetTalk thread for followers specifically interested in discussing the latest devices.

Promote Networking

- Encourage members to collaborate, share resources, or support each other's projects.

Example: A writing coach might create a thread where aspiring authors can connect and share feedback on each other's work.

11.6 Gathering and Acting on Feedback

Feedback is a valuable tool for understanding your audience's needs and improving the community experience.

Conduct Surveys

- Use polls or surveys to gather insights into audience preferences, concerns, and suggestions.
- Keep questions focused and actionable.

Example: "What type of content would you like to see more of? Vote below:

Tutorals

Behind-the-scenes

Polls and Q&As."

Implement Suggestions

- Act on constructive feedback to show members that their opinions are valued.
- Highlight changes or improvements based on community input.

Example: "Thanks to your feedback, we're launching a weekly poll series to make this space even more interactive!"

11.7 Monitoring Community Health

Regularly assessing your community's health ensures its long-term success and sustainability.

Track Engagement Metrics

- Analyze participation rates, content shares, and growth trends using X Analytics or third-party tools.
- Look for patterns to understand what types of content or interactions drive the most engagement.

Example: If polls consistently outperform other posts, consider increasing their frequency.

Address Issues Promptly

- Resolve conflicts, moderate negative behaviors, and address harmful comments swiftly to maintain a positive environment.
- Use tools like muting, blocking, or reporting for persistent violations of guidelines.

Tip: Regularly review your community standards to ensure they remain relevant and effective.

Conclusion

Building and managing a thriving community on X requires a thoughtful approach that prioritizes inclusivity, engagement, and value. By fostering connections, recognizing contributions, and acting on feedback, you can create a supportive space where members feel valued and motivated to participate. In the next chapter, we'll explore strategies for scaling your efforts and adapting to changes in X's features and policies to sustain growth over time.

Chapter 12: Navigating Challenges and Mitigating Risks on X

Building a presence on X offers exciting opportunities to grow, engage, and monetize, but it also comes with challenges and risks. From managing negative interactions to safeguarding your mental well-being, addressing these obstacles effectively is crucial for sustaining a positive experience on the platform. This chapter provides actionable strategies to overcome common challenges and minimize risks.

12.1 Managing Negative Interactions

As your presence on X grows, you may encounter trolls, harassment, or unconstructive feedback. Handling these interactions thoughtfully is key to maintaining a healthy online environment.

Trolls and Harassment

- Use X's features to block or mute accounts that engage in disruptive behavior.
- Report violations such as hate speech, threats, or harassment to X for further action.
- Avoid engaging with trolls, as responses often escalate conflicts.

Example: If someone repeatedly posts inflammatory comments, block the account and report it for violating X's guidelines.

Constructive Criticism vs. Negativity

- Distinguish between valid critiques and unwarranted negativity.
- Engage constructively with feedback that is helpful and ignore or mute baseless criticism.

Example: A follower pointing out an error in your post provides an opportunity to acknowledge and correct it, demonstrating accountability.

12.2 Protecting Your Account

Your X account is the cornerstone of your presence on the platform, and securing it is essential to prevent unauthorized access or data breaches.

Security Measures

- Enable **two-factor authentication** (2FA) for added security.
- Regularly update your password, ensuring it is strong and unique.
- Monitor account activity for any suspicious logins or changes.

Tip: Use a password manager to store and create complex passwords securely.

Privacy Settings

- Adjust your account settings to control who can view your posts, reply to your tweets, or tag you.
- For sensitive topics or personal safety concerns, consider limiting audience visibility or enabling private mode.

Example: A creator discussing controversial topics might restrict replies to followers only, reducing exposure to trolls.

12.3 Avoiding Content Violations

Maintaining compliance with X's content policies is crucial to avoid penalties, such as post removals or account suspension.

Adherence to Guidelines

- Familiarize yourself with X's policies on prohibited content, including hate speech, misinformation, and unmarked sensitive media.
- Use appropriate labels for posts containing adult or sensitive material.

Intellectual Property

- Ensure you have the rights to share any content, including images, videos, or quotes.
- Always credit creators when sharing their work to avoid infringement claims.

Example: If reposting a graphic from another user, tag their account and confirm their permission when required.

12.4 Handling Misinformation

Sharing accurate information is vital for maintaining credibility and trust with your audience.

Fact-Checking

- Verify sources before sharing news, statistics, or claims.
- Cross-check with reputable outlets or primary sources to ensure accuracy.

Corrections

- If you share incorrect information, promptly issue a correction. Acknowledge the mistake transparently to uphold audience trust.

Example: "Correction: In my earlier post, I mentioned [incorrect fact]. The correct information is [accurate fact]. Thank you for pointing this out."

12.5 Balancing Engagement and Well-being

Active engagement is important, but maintaining your mental health and avoiding burnout are equally critical for long-term success.

Avoiding Burnout

- Set boundaries for your time on X. Use scheduling tools to automate posts and reduce the need for constant presence.
- Schedule regular breaks from social media to recharge and focus on offline activities.

Tip: Designate "digital detox" days to refresh your perspective and creativity.

Mental Health

- Be mindful of the emotional impact of negative interactions or overexposure to stressful content.
- Seek support from friends, family, or mental health professionals if needed.

Example: If a post receives overwhelming negativity, step back temporarily to regain perspective before addressing the situation.

12.6 Navigating Algorithm Changes

X's algorithms directly affect content visibility and engagement. Adapting to updates ensures you stay relevant and maintain your reach.

Staying Informed

- Follow X's official accounts and updates to stay informed about algorithm changes.
- Join creator communities or forums where others discuss and share strategies for adapting to updates.

Adaptability

- Experiment with different content types and posting times to identify what works best under the new algorithm.

- Monitor analytics closely to track shifts in engagement and adjust your strategy accordingly.

Example: If text-based posts receive reduced visibility due to algorithm changes, shift focus to multimedia content or interactive formats like polls.

Conclusion

Navigating challenges on X requires preparation, adaptability, and a proactive mindset. By managing negative interactions, protecting your account, and prioritizing your well-being, you can mitigate risks and maintain a positive presence on the platform. Additionally, staying informed and flexible in response to algorithm changes ensures your continued growth and success. In the next chapter, we'll explore advanced strategies for scaling your efforts and achieving long-term sustainability on X.

Chapter 13: Staying Informed and Adapting to Platform Changes

The digital landscape is constantly evolving, and platforms like X are no exception. To maintain and grow your presence effectively, it's crucial to stay informed about updates, policy changes, and new features while adapting your strategies to align with these shifts. This chapter outlines actionable methods to stay ahead of platform changes and integrate them into your content approach for sustained success.

13.1 Monitoring Platform Updates

Staying informed about X's latest developments ensures you're never caught off guard by changes that could impact your strategy.

Official Channels

- Regularly check X's **official blog** and **help center** for announcements about:
    - New features or tools.
    - Changes to policies or guidelines.
    - Algorithm updates affecting content visibility.
- Follow X's official social media accounts for real-time updates and insights.

Example: If X announces a new ad revenue model, learning about it early allows you to adjust your content and monetization strategies promptly.

Industry News

- Stay connected to reputable tech news outlets such as **TechCrunch**, **The Verge**, or **Social Media Today** for expert analyses and detailed reports on platform changes.
- Follow industry analysts and thought leaders who specialize in social media trends.

Tip: Set up Google Alerts or use RSS feeds to receive timely updates about X and other social media platforms.

13.2 Engaging with the Community

Leveraging the knowledge and experiences of fellow creators can provide valuable insights into adapting to platform changes.

Forums and Groups

- Join online communities on platforms like **Reddit**, **Discord**, or **Facebook Groups** where creators discuss:
  - Experiences with new features.
  - Insights into recent policy changes.
  - Best practices for adapting to updates.

Example: A group for X creators might share tips on maximizing engagement with a newly introduced content format.

Networking

- Connect with other content creators, either within your niche or in broader creator communities.
- Exchange strategies, share lessons learned, and collaborate to test new tools or features.

Tip: Networking isn't just about learning—it can also spark new collaboration opportunities, helping both parties grow.

13.3 Experimenting with New Features

Adopting new features early can give you a competitive edge, helping you stand out and capture attention.

Early Adoption

- Experiment with new tools or features as soon as they're introduced.
- Test different approaches to understand how these features can best serve your content strategy.

Example: If X rolls out a feature allowing creators to host paid Spaces, you could test it by hosting an exclusive workshop or Q&A session for your audience.

Feedback Loop

- Ask your audience for feedback on your use of new features or formats.
- Use polls, comments, or direct messages to gauge their interest and adjust your strategy accordingly.

Tip: Encourage honest feedback by framing questions like, "What did you think of this format? Would you like to see more of this type of content?"

13.4 Analyzing Performance Metrics

Data is your best tool for understanding the impact of changes and fine-tuning your approach.

Data-Driven Decisions

- Use X Analytics to monitor key performance indicators (KPIs) such as:
    - Engagement rates.
    - Reach and impressions.
    - Follower growth trends.
- Pay attention to metrics before and after significant platform updates to identify their impact.

Example: If a new algorithm favors video content, you might notice a spike in engagement for tweets containing videos compared to text-only posts.

Trend Identification

- Look for patterns in audience behavior, such as increased interaction with specific content types or formats.
- Use these insights to refine your content and posting schedule.

13.5 Adapting Content Strategies

Flexibility and continuous learning are key to thriving on a platform as dynamic as X.

Flexibility

- Be prepared to adjust your content plan to align with platform updates or shifts in audience engagement.
- Stay open to experimenting with new formats or topics, even if they're outside your usual comfort zone.

Example: If X's algorithm starts prioritizing interactive posts, such as polls or live sessions, incorporate these into your regular schedule.

Continuous Learning

- Dedicate time to learning about new tools, techniques, and best practices for content creation and audience engagement.
- Attend webinars, workshops, or industry events focused on social media trends and innovations.

Tip: Follow creators or educators who specialize in teaching the latest social media strategies to stay updated and inspired.

Conclusion

Navigating the ever-changing landscape of X requires vigilance, adaptability, and a willingness to experiment. By staying informed about platform updates, engaging with the creator community, and using data to refine your approach, you can ensure sustained growth and relevance. Adapting quickly to changes not only helps maintain engagement but also positions you as a leader in your niche, capable of thriving in a dynamic digital environment.

Chapter 14: Case Studies of Successful Monetization on X

Examining real-world examples of creators who have effectively monetized their presence on X provides valuable insights and practical strategies. This chapter showcases diverse approaches to financial success on the platform while highlighting actionable strategies to achieve significant milestones, such as 5 million impressions in 30 days.

Strategies for Achieving 5 Million Impressions in 30 Days

Achieving 5 million impressions in a month requires a combination of strategic planning, content optimization, and audience engagement. Here are proven strategies with real-world examples:

1. Create Viral Threads

Threads with valuable, shareable insights tend to attract high engagement, significantly boosting impressions.

- **Strategy**: Break down complex topics into easy-to-follow points. Use hooks to grab attention and visuals to enhance clarity.
- **Example**: A digital marketer posted a thread titled, *"10 Proven Social Media Strategies to Skyrocket Your Growth"*, which included actionable tips and visuals. It gained over 1 million impressions within a week.

2. Leverage Trending Topics

Participating in trending conversations or hashtags can expose your content to a broader audience.

- **Strategy**: Monitor trends relevant to your niche and contribute meaningful insights or commentary.
- **Example**: A fitness influencer joined the #WorldHealthDay conversation by sharing "5 Quick Exercises to Boost Energy Levels," incorporating videos and a poll. This tweet garnered 500,000 impressions in a single day.

3. Collaborate with Influencers

Partnering with larger accounts amplifies your reach and introduces your content to new audiences.

- **Strategy**: Co-author posts, host joint Spaces, or share each other's tweets.
- **Example**: A personal finance coach collaborated with a popular economist to create a joint thread on "Recession-Proof Savings Tips," generating 2 million impressions from shared audiences.

4. Post High-Engagement Formats

Content like polls, videos, and infographics typically drive higher interaction, increasing impressions.

- **Strategy**: Use polls to encourage participation and videos to communicate complex ideas succinctly.
- **Example**: A tech reviewer created a poll asking, *"What's the best smartphone of 2024?"* alongside a comparison video. The poll received thousands of votes and impressions from retweets.

5. Schedule Consistent Posting Times

Consistency keeps your audience engaged and increases visibility through the algorithm.

- **Strategy**: Use analytics to determine peak times when your audience is most active.
- **Example**: A travel blogger posted daily sunrise photos with motivational quotes at 7 a.m. EST, gaining predictable engagement that led to over 5 million impressions in 30 days.

6. Engage Directly with Followers

Replying to comments and participating in discussions boosts visibility for your posts.

- **Strategy**: Ask open-ended questions and respond to replies thoughtfully.
- **Example**: A business coach tweeted, *"What's the best career advice you've ever received? Let's discuss!"* The replies sparked conversations, amplifying impressions as followers engaged.

Case Studies of Successful Monetization on X

Case Study 1: The Tech Enthusiast

- **Profile**: A technology blogger specializing in gadget reviews and industry news.
- **Monetization Strategies**:
    - Affiliate Marketing: Shared product links, earning commissions on sales.
    - Sponsored Content: Partnered with tech brands for paid reviews.
    - Creator Subscriptions: Offered exclusive early access to reviews.
- **Outcome**: Created a steady income stream by diversifying revenue sources while maintaining authenticity.

Case Study 2: The Fitness Coach

- **Profile**: A certified trainer sharing workouts, nutrition advice, and motivational posts.
- **Monetization Strategies**:
    - Online Coaching: Promoted personalized training programs.
    - Digital Products: Sold e-books and meal plans via direct links.
    - Brand Partnerships: Partnered with fitness brands for sponsored posts.
- **Outcome**: Built a loyal community, driving product sales and securing long-term brand deals.

Case Study 3: The Visual Artist

- **Profile**: An illustrator showcasing original artwork and behind-the-scenes videos.
- **Monetization Strategies**:
    - Print Sales: Marketed art prints and merchandise via an online store.
    - Crowdfunding: Used Patreon to offer exclusive content and process videos.
    - Workshops: Conducted virtual art tutorials.
- **Outcome**: Created multiple income streams, enabling financial growth and recognition in the art community.

Case Study 4: The Culinary Influencer

- **Profile**: A food enthusiast sharing recipes, cooking tips, and reviews.
- **Monetization Strategies**:
    - Ad Revenue Sharing: Earned from engaging posts viewed by Premium users.
    - Sponsored Content: Collaborated with food brands for recipe promotions.
    - Affiliate Marketing: Shared links to kitchen gadgets and ingredients.
- **Outcome**: Balanced ad revenue, sponsorships, and affiliate income while maintaining audience trust.

Key Takeaways

1. **Diversification**
   Implementing multiple monetization strategies provides financial stability and growth opportunities.
2. **Authenticity**
   Building trust with your audience is essential for long-term success. Transparent, genuine interactions foster loyalty and engagement.
3. **Adaptability**
   Being open to new opportunities and pivoting strategies based on data or platform changes can significantly enhance results.

4. **Consistency**
   Regular, high-quality content paired with strategic engagement is key to achieving milestones like 5 million impressions in a month.

Conclusion

These case studies and strategies highlight the diverse ways creators can achieve financial success and significant growth on X. With creativity, strategic planning, and consistent effort, the platform offers endless possibilities for monetization across various niches and content types. The journey requires persistence and adaptability, but the rewards are well worth the effort.